The Sit N Do Nothing Series

Hamsters Unite-Relationships Workbook

Volume Four of
The Sit 'N' Do Nothing
Hamster Series

Humans All Make Some Time Exploring Relationships

Written By Wendy Proteau

The Sit N Do Nothing Series

Covers designed by: Wendy Proteau

Copyright2009©WendyProteau
All Rights Reserved
TXU001655158

The Sit N Do Nothing Series

The Committed Hamsters

Here you are the happy little couple. It doesn't matter if you've been together a year or seventy…this book is for everyone in a relationship or living together. How did it all happen? Where did you find one another? How do you live? Ever stop to reflect on it all? I'm betting your life is busy. You worked hard to get here. You may have children and you're busy running a home, extra-curricular activities, sports, etc…so many things to keep up with.

You're holding this book and it could be a gift from a family member, best friend, a couple you know or even a curious neighbor. Maybe you've picked it up for something to do on your flight celebrating your 3rd honeymoon. Who knows the why, but you're here. These are straightforward shoot from the hip questions we often don't think about during daily life.

You both are an accumulation of every moment you've experienced up until this point. You've lived, laughed, learned and grew as a couple. So let's focus on the two of you for a while. These aren't hard questions and they cover a variety of topics. Some will make you giggle and some may even surprise you, but I want you have fun with this all. We've been on this earth together for thousands of years yet, men are men and women are women. How often do you shake your head at what the partner does or says? You get it right back, don't ya?

Do you talk about all the lil things you've done or gone through? Do you admit to the mistakes, glory in the successes, share past memories? Maybe you do, maybe you don't…

With the world moving so fast, it's a wonder you ever get time to connect with your spouse. It took two people to make your relationship, so it will take both to fill in the questions. Let's just stop for a moment and reflect on your life together. There is just one rule to this book

"GOTTA BE HONEST!"

The Sit N Do Nothing Series

Partner Hamster Basics

Little known facts about_____ and _____
                          (first name)   (first name)

Today's date is: _____

Our last name_____

We live at _____

But we have also lived together: (last address)

_____

This book was given to us by_____

In 5 words we would describe our relationship as a couple

1_____

2_____

3_____

4_____

5_____

In 5 words we would describe the person/people who gave us this as

1_____

2_____

3_____

4_____

5_____

The Sit N Do Nothing Series

Her information:

Born _____ day _____ month _____ year

Born in_____ Time she was born_____

Raised in_____

Her education level is _____

She went to the following schools-name and year please:

_____

_____

_____

She works as a_____

And as been at her current job _____years

Has worked in her field for _____years

The Sit N Do Nothing Series

His information:

Born _____ day _____ month _____ year

Born in_____ Time he was born _____

Raised in_____

Education level is _____

He went to the following schools-name and year please:

_____

_____

_____

He works as a_____

And as been at his current job _____years

Has worked in his field for _____years

See, not so hard is it…..
SO LET'S START HAVING SOME FUN!

The Sit N Do Nothing Series

THE COMMITTED RELATIONSHIP HAMSTERS

Volume Four

Well here you both are…the partners! I must congratulate you on finding your significant other, better half, equal, however you wish to express it. Remember the single days and trying to find that magical connection? Well you've done it!

Let's think way back to before you got married or started living together. You were obviously both looking for a partner in life and had priorities and preferences. I want you to think back to the first moment you met your partner.

1-How did you manage to meet each other, was this

____A blind date   ____Date site match   ____Friend of a friend

____Family occasion   ____Through work   ____A set up by family

____A chance meeting   ____Set up by a friend   ____ While shopping

If other, please explain: _____

Where did you first see each other _____

2-Ok, so wherever it was, sparks flew-Woo hoo! Let's ask the basics.

Who noticed who first

_____

And I guess someone took the initiative to start contact.

Who was it that reached out first   Him_____ Her_____

Was it immediate or did they try to make you notice them?

_____

What was the opening line

_____

Who got the phone number to call each other first?

        He got hers _____ She got his _____

Now scenarios are far too many to list here as yes or no questions, so I'm going to presume the conversations began and things flowed to the point of the first date. So let's ask these just to narrow it down a bit:

How long from:

First contact to first phone call _____ hrs/day/week/month

First contact to actual date _____ hrs/day/week/month

Who made the plan for the first date _____

How long did the first date last _____

3-Okay so we got a basis for what happened at the start. Now for the first date I have to ask the following:

What day of the week was it _____

Check off which one applied to your situation:

Did you meet at mutual location   _____

Did he pick you up at your door   _____

Did you pick him up at his place   _____

So however it happened, you're now going to be standing face to face on your first date. Yikes! Thrills, excitement, nerves...so how long did it take each of you to get ready for that date:

She took _____ minutes/hours   He took _____ minutes/hours

She changed clothes _____ times   He changed clothes _____ times

Were you nervous before hand   Him: ___yes ___no   Her: ___yes ___no

Let's see how well each of you remember that night by answering what your partner was wearing that night. Now he fills in what she wore and vice versa:

She was wearing _____

He was wearing _____

4- Standing there looking at each other, the stomach is doing flip-flops and your both checking each other out. Go back to the very first impressions of that moment. Below there is a list of possible things flitting through your head at that very first moment. I want you put a check mark for each first impression. W is for the ladies and M for the men's thoughts. Now not all will apply-just mark the one's that do. (Her answers under the W, his under the M) Picture it, you are face to face and:

	W	M
I like what I see	___	___
They look nervous	___	___
Look at that smile	___	___
I'm so attracted to them	___	___
I'm fidgeting	___	___
Why am I so nervous	___	___
What if we don't click	___	___
They look so at ease	___	___
I have butterflies	___	___
I hope I don't sound like a dork	___	___
I will just follow the lead	___	___
Don't know if I like them	___	___
I'm calm, cool, collected	___	___

This is gonna be fun   _____   _____

Wonder what they kiss like   _____   _____

Really not my type   _____   _____

5-We get past the initial nerves and you're off…so your first date was where:
_____

Anything disastrous happen (spilled drink, bad food, car problems)
_____

Now that night after the date, you probably thought about how it all went, so on a scale from 1-10 rate your date as a whole. Not everyone has a perfect first date…rarely does anything run smoothly in life, huh? (1 being-yikes, 10 being the ultimate)

She thinks it was a _____   He thinks it was a _____

Well no matter what the first one was, obviously many dates followed or you wouldn't be doing the married/relationship book now would you.

So let's see if you remember:

2nd date we did: _____

3rd date we did: _____

4rth date we did: _____

And then there is that first kiss moment. Let's remember back to that very first time and in one word describe that first kiss:

He thought the kiss was _____

She thought the kiss was_____

Now with the dating process, you go out several times and then that magical moment comes along, the intimacy. Let's find out about the first time:

The Sit N Do Nothing Series

Day of the week was _____ After date #_____

It happened where?

_____

6-So when did you know that you had found the perfect partner for life? How long did it take you to figure it all out?

Her _____ days/months/years　　　　　　　　Him_____ days/months/years

7-Looking back over your previous dating history of others, something must have stood out about this one from all the rest. We all go through trials and errors and we think we know what we want and what we are physically attracted to, yet sometimes we fall for something totally different. So we ask this question.

Was your spouse normally what you would have been attracted to?

He says ___yes ____no

What was physically different about her

_____

She says ___yes ____no

What was physically different about him

_____

This next part is the whole living together/wedding thing. Some questions will apply to the living together situation-some to the wedding. Answer what ya can.

8-If you are married, we have the proposal. Some are downright romantic, some are traditional and some are ordinary. There is no right way, it's as individual as the people in the relationship and today women initiate things as well. It could be you decided to live together first and that was the first big question.

How was the proposal done/what was the approach for moving in together

_____

_____

Was it a surprise ____yes ____no

How long after you met _____days/months/years

I wonder did the person initiating let anyone in on the plan, I mean I would probably talk to a friend or family member if I was considering a big step. So for whoever did the asking….

Did you talk to anyone first _____yes _____no Who was it_____

What was their initial reaction

_____

If marriage, how long did you wait to ask from the time you bought the ring?

_____ days/months/years

How long did it take you to come up with how to propose _____ days/months/years

9-I guess I'd be worried if I had to propose to someone or take the next big step of living together…think I'd be scared they'd say no. For the person who did the asking-

Did you ever think they might have declined   ____yes ____no

Did you talk to their parents first   ____yes ____no

If so, on a scale of 1-10…(10 being they were thrilled about it)

Her parent's response was a _____   His parent's response was a _____

I guess this all lead to the wedding plans. Were ya on the same page? Let's find out.

PLANNING THE WEDDING-for those who've done it or those who are planning to do it:

Now weddings are a bunch of intricate plans to pull off all in a certain amount of time. There are choices, deadlines, preferences and so much to contend with. Some people keep it simple, while some are elaborate. (The W is for her answers and M is for his)

	W	M
I wanted a big wedding	___	___
I wanted a small affair	___	___
I wanted to elope	___	___
I prefer a justice of the peace	___	___

Now often one makes a lot of the decisions, at times, it's a collaborated effort. So we will leave the two columns as they are, but if you both agreed equally (no fighting about it) use the column under B for both. (If you're not married, you can skip to question 12)

I had most of the say in the:

	W	M	B
Food	___	___	___
Flowers	___	___	___
Place	___	___	___
Cake	___	___	___
Decorations	___	___	___
Photographer	___	___	___
Tuxedo	___	___	___
Wedding gown	___	___	___
Music	___	___	___

I had most of the say in the:

	W	M	B
Guest list	____	____	____
Color scheme	____	____	____
Ceremony	____	____	____
Minister	____	____	____
Actual date	____	____	____

Wow, that's a lot to go through, isn't it and I'm sure it was time consuming yet beautiful. Were there some difficult moments through it all? No matter how well you plan, at times things just happen.

Was there anything that didn't run "smooth as silk" on that day?

_____

_____

No matter what happened…you met your equal in life, nothing compares to that really. So let's ask each of you, if you could go back and re-plan your wedding would you maybe choose something totally different knowing what you do now? (Maybe marry on a beach instead?)

He would_____

She would_____

10-This depends on how long ago you were married. I've watched TV shows about weddings nowadays and they can sky rocket to unreal costs.

So let's have it…what did your wedding cost $_____ just bottom total.

If you're planning on getting married, what figure are you putting aside for the big event?

Our budget for our wedding will be around $_____

11- Now the honeymoon! I never understood that honeymoon concept...does going away make a difference? Is it like a time of peace and enjoyment before the real world? I never did get that. I was married once and we went fishing for a weekend, it was cold, rainy and not romantic. Nothing says romance like a Walleye!

Where did you honeymoon _____

How long was it _____

Was it romantic _____ Any fish involved_____ (I just had to)

Who planned the honeymoon _____

Would you go there again on an anniversary _____

Cohabitating or married these will all apply-committed is committed!

12-You're together now and waking up beside your partner for the first time. These questions may pertain to the living together stage or the after married stage. There is always an adjustment period when you first move in.

So we are going to ask: What was the one thing that was hard for you to get used to waking up to each other? It could be anything from the cold feet on your legs, the snoring, covers stolen, the waking up with an arm over your head:

For her _____

For him _____

With the one thing that was hard to get used to, there is the one thing that you loved waking up beside them for, that cute smile, their hair all tousled, their sleepy morning ways.

For her _____

For him _____

How long did it take for you to get used to each other, where it just felt comfortable for you both:

Took him _____ days/months _____ still adjusting

Took him _____ days/months _____ still adjusting

13- As time goes by you have to get used to each other's 'lil' differences. Everyone has a different way of doing things and sometimes there are just those lil things that drive you nuts the first while.

Let's check off the one's that applied to you. Some may have bothered one or the other and you know you talked about it for the first while. (W is for the women to mark if it bothered them and, M is the man's) Check off all that applied:

	W	M
Schedule differences	_____	_____
Morning ritual differences	_____	_____
Toilet seat issues	_____	_____
Toothpaste squeezing	_____	_____
Cooking habits	_____	_____
Cleaning habits	_____	_____
Organizing things	_____	_____
Each other's stuff in the way	_____	_____
Way you do laundry	_____	_____
Leaving things in the wrong place	_____	_____
Not picking up your stuff	_____	_____
Repairing things	_____	_____
Letting each other know plans	_____	_____

The Sit N Do Nothing Series

Forgetting to do things _____   _____

Privacy   _____   _____

14- Those are things that you go through when putting two people in the same close quarters. Some people adapt easily while others still have issues. Is there one thing that you've just had to get used to since it's never changed over the course of the years and probably never will? (list 3 each)

For him:

_____

_____

_____

For her:

_____

_____

_____

15- Some things just won't change, but it's all good once you let it go, isn't it? Being together and sharing a home you must work well together or you wouldn't be doing this book. Think over some of the things you've had to work on together and state who is the stronger on each of these topics. Now here it's one or the other. Check-off under the appropriate column, who is better at (The W for she's strong at, the M for he rules that department)

	W	M
Home decorating	____	____
Building things	____	____
Electrical repair	____	____
Furniture decisions	____	____
Painting	____	____

The Sit N Do Nothing Series

	W	M
Yard work	____	____
Gardening	____	____
Car maintenance	____	____
Plumbing	____	____
Renovations	____	____
Following a plan	____	____

We'll cover more of these later….this is just the start of sharing in a relationship.

16-Let's think on some fun things, shall we? Couples you hang out with all the time-the best of friends who enjoy doing things with you as couples. Think back to when you were first married and all the other couples you knew back then, do you still associate with any of them?

How many couples from way back _____

How many new couple friends have you made over the time _____

Who is your favorite couple to do things with?_____ and _____

How often do you see them _____ /week/month/year

So you must all watch each other's relationship/marriages grow and change. Sometimes we bounce ideas off one another and learn by watching them. So out of all the couples you know, family, friends etc… who's marriage/relationship would you say yours is most like, in that you seem to experience a lot of the same things as they do.

_____ and _____

17-Now you both had friends before you were married and I'm sure you didn't always click with each other's friends, so who was it that you just didn't like around your spouse.

She just absolutely didn't like his friend _____

He just couldn't stand her friend _____

So what happened to those people I wonder? Do you still keep in contact occasionally or are they distant memories?

Did he give up his friend _____yes _____no

Did she give up her friend _____yes _____no

Even now you may have friends that don't seem to mesh well with your spouse. You know the ones-"honey (so and so) is coming over tonight…and you just see the eye roll happening from your partner. Now it's not that there not good friends or good people-just you like them and your spouse-not so much.

So those current friends would be:

His friends_____

Her friends_____

But you go along with it and I'm sure do your best, love's about give n take.

18-Here's something to think on…I want you each to list the top 5 things about being with your spouse. It could be he's a fabulous cook or she is a terrific bargain hunter. Those 'lil' things that you just appreciate so much about having each other:

Her list	His list
_____	_____
_____	_____
_____	_____
_____	_____
_____	_____

19-What are the most attractive things about your spouse? We all have many physical traits, but some stand out above the rest. I know you love everything about your spouse, but number these, 1-12, (#1 being the best thing all the way to 12) that you just find so attractive. Ladies mark your 1-12 under the W and men mark yours under the M.

	W	M		W	M
Eyes	___	___	Hair	___	___
Legs	___	___	Butt	___	___
Arm	___	___	Waist	___	___
Chest	___	___	Feet	___	___
Hands	___	___	Smile	___	___
Lips	___	___	Nose	___	___

20-This one is playful, what cartoon character does your partner most resemble in appearance:

He thinks she looks like: _____

She thinks he looks like: _____

What cartoon character would your partner say you most acts like at times Could be the way they talk, walk, decision making, creative solutions etc…

He thinks she acts most like:

_____

She thinks he acts most like:

_____

Ok you're both giggling I hope. Tis fun to think on crazy things! Nothing says love like laughing together. So let's try it again and keep this in context as gentle teasing please.

People have a way of doing normal everyday things, like mowing the grass a certain way, cooking style, even personal grooming habits. You've probably kidded each other or shook your head at some of their ways, because it just doesn't seem to work out the way they planned or made sense to you. If you had to give your spouse a nickname to suit what they can't do: (examples: wondering-plumber, cooks-no-more, reno reject)

For her he would say _____

For him she would say _____

Keep smiling-partnership is about having a best friend to give you a hard time with a smile, sometimes.

21-While we're thinking on the subject of things that just make you shake your head, let's think way back n the day…long, long ago, when life wasn't so easy. Back when marriages sometimes were arranged over long distances. At times, you never even met your spouse before the wedding day and when you did, you set out on the frontier to forge your way all on your own. Let's picture you in those days, how do you think you would have done as a couple with those odds? Think of the following and simply rate on a scale from 1 to five how your partner would do (#1 being no problem for them to adapt, 5 being no way they'd ever make it) Ladies use the M column for your thoughts on how he would do, gents under the W on how she would fare:

	W	M
Not meeting before marrying	___	___
Months of travel by horse n carriage	___	___
Building your own wood/sod house	___	___
Working from sun up to sun down	___	___
Outhouse	___	___
Carrying water from the stream/heating it for a bath	___	___
Contact only once in a while with family (letters took a long time back then)	___	___
Spending most of your time by yourselves (neighbor is a day ride away)	___	___
Sleeping on a straw mattress	___	___

The Sit N Do Nothing Series

	W	M
Raising farm animals	___	___
Preserving your own food	___	___
Hunting/trapping for fresh meat	___	___
Preparing, skinning the meat (ewe)	___	___
No hospitals-handling it on your own	___	___
Spouse being gone at times for months (work often separated people)	___	___
Home births	___	___
Making all your own clothes	___	___
Washing clothes in the river	___	___
Buying supplies only 2-3 times a year	___	___
Building with no power tools	___	___
Raising kids in a 2-3 room house at times	___	___
Milking cows	___	___

That was a long time ago, but it really makes you appreciate the times we live in, doesn't it. Can't imagine living without a lot of the conveniences we have now.

22-Now we're going to move on to children. Some relationships even have combined families with children from previous relationships. Some couples are just starting out raising children, while others have grown children already.

Part A, will be for people who are the biological parents together and **Part B** for blended/combined families. Some may apply to both...never know!

A-Biological Parents

How many children do you have together _____

How many boys _____   How many girls _____

Who picked their names? We both agreed on them _____yes _____ no

He picked #_____ of names   She picked # of _____names

I know there is no such thing as favorites, but at times children just gravitate more towards one parent or the other. Not that you love them any differently…just the children seem closer with one or the other. Now I don't know how children you have, I hope I left enough room so you can list them in the proper spaces.

Definitely more attached to dad would be:

_____ _____ _____ _____

Definitely more attached to mom would be:

_____ _____ _____ _____

If you're just married and starting out, are you planning on having kids? How many

       He wants _____   She wants_____

Does each of you have names already lined up? I know I've always favored certain names throughout life.

What are names she likes _____ _____ _____

What are names he likes _____ _____ _____

What attributes would you like each of them to have? I know when I was married a long time ago I wanted children to have my humor…it could be temperament, looks, habits etc…you must have some wishes.

She would like if her children had his:

_____

He would like if his children had her:

_____

B- (the combined family questions)

How many kids do you have all together _____

How many boys_____

How many girls_____

Names please: (I left extra room in case you need more spaces)

Girls: _____ _____ _____ _____

Boys: _____ _____ _____ _____

Do they all get along with each other _____yes _____ no _____ getting there

Being a combined family would have more challenges I would think. Two sets of parents, two separate styles of parenting, definitely not an easy task…yet it could work out way better! I remember fighting with my siblings because we were so much alike. It's only in the later years we recognized we got along well. With combined families, I think they could be best of friends.

So the hardest part about combining your two families was:

_____

_____

Who most surprised you, with how they get along?

_____ and _____

Now looking at all the kids, have they gotten traits from the step parents? Are they learning new things from either step parent?

He believes his children have learned the following from their step mom

_____

_____

She believes her children have learned the following from their step father

_____

_____

23-Well on to fun partner stuff you do together. Those moments when you just get to have fun as a couple. I know for my sister and her hubby, it's golfing together, that's their favorite outing. So let's ask you, which do you normally enjoy? Mark with A,B,C etc…in order of preference (A is #1 choice)

Dining out	_____ Golfing	_____
Attending sporting event	_____ Ballet	_____
Theatre	_____ Symphony	_____
Live concert	_____ Sailing	_____
Movie night	_____ Rock climbing/hiking	_____
Bonfires	_____ Attending a party	_____
Gambling/casino	_____ Going for walks	_____
Swimming/Laying on a beach	_____ Fishing	_____
Boating-water ski	_____	

Did I miss some? Please add if I did.

_____ _____ _____ _____ _____

You do your favorite at least _____ times per month.

24-Now I'm sure you've dreamed of travel or perhaps you're avid travelers already. What is the one place you'd love to both go if it were all paid for you?

_____

Is there one place you've been that you just both fell in love with?

Where _____ When did you go _____

25-Given the opportunity to do anything with your spouse, check off what you'd love to try together, just once. You have to agree on these since you'd have to do them together.

Bungee jump	_____	Sky dive	_____
Deep-sea fish	_____	Mountain climb	_____
Cliff dive	_____	Spa day together	_____
Hot air balloon ride	_____	Dude ranch	_____
Trip to South Pole	_____	African safari	_____
Explore the Amazon	_____	Dive with the Sharks	_____

Perhaps you've done a lot of these things already. Some people are adventurers…while some just play it safe.

26-Since you've been together, do you have nicknames for each other? I know couples use the cutest names sometimes. (Dumpling, Buttercup, Sugarplum, Sunshine)
Please do share them.

Her favorite nickname for him is _____

His favorite nickname for her is _____

27-Now nicknames are cute, but ya know sometimes they have one name just to get under your skin. They smirk afterwards, but you just hate them calling you that little pet name, don't ya?

Pet name that just gets under her skin is _____

Pet name that just gets under his skin is _____

28-If you were forced to go back and live one year as a couple in a historic times, what era would you choose to go back and live in: examples-Age of the Dinosaurs, Roman Empire or Revolutionary war. You probably have different thoughts, but you have to choose only one as a couple, because your being put in the time machine together whether you like it or not. Think seriously what era would you decide and why?

Era_____

Why
_____

_____

_____

Now depending on the time you chose you'd both have a different type of life, different roles or occupation. So thinking back to that time-what would you think your spouse would have been back then?

He thinks she would have been a _____

She thinks he would have been a _____

29-What personality traits shine the strongest in each of you? Characteristics are hard to miss-they make us who we are and not just when dealing with each other, but when in the world around you. You appreciate each other or you wouldn't be together, so let's gauge it all, who shows the following more strongly. Put a W if it is more prevalent in her or an M if it's in him. You can use an E, only if you both agree you're on equal footing in that department.

Humor	_____	Nurturing	_____
Expressive	_____	Talkative	_____
Shy	_____	Outgoing	_____
Laid back	_____	Street smart	_____
Book smart	_____	Worrying	_____
Work ethic	_____	Athleticism	_____
Public speaking	_____	Leader	_____
Follower	_____	Inventive	_____
Crafty	_____	Romantic	_____
Honest	_____	Trusting	_____
Stubborn	_____	Artistic	_____
Following instructions	_____	Career	_____
Accomplishing tasks	_____	Money management	_____
Goal planning	_____	Mechanical ability	_____
Planning	_____	Frugal/spendthrift	_____
Emotional strength	_____	Intellectual strength	_____
Decisiveness	_____	Attention lover	_____

Every couple has its combination that works. What one may be strong in, they may lack in another area or at times be totally equal. It's the balance that makes it all work.

30-Now every couple uses the barter system. I have watched over the years and many say, "I'll do that, if you do this." It's rather unique how people trade off, so let's ask you both if you had something you wanted to do and you knew your partner will say "no way", what would you be willing to barter in order to get them to sway them in your direction? Think on the biggest bargaining chip you have, because you know they're going to dig in their heels, AND it's a once in a lifetime event that you really want.

She would be willing to

_____

_____

He would be willing to

_____

_____

31-Habits, habits, habits…and if you've been together for a while-yep, you both got them and some you wish you could change about your partner. List the top 3 things that you just wish your partner would change once and for all.

His wish list

_____

_____

_____

Her wish list

_____

_____

_____

That probably came easy for both of you, whether it was smoking, socks on the floor, messy when they cook…whatever it was you know it makes you crazy.

32-On that same line of thinking, they say we women meet hoping to change the man and men meet hoping we women never change. That may explain the difference in the sexes over the years. Rather profound really. Really think about it, what are the top 3 things you hope never changes about your partner.

His wish list

_____

_____

_____

Her wish list

_____

_____

_____

33-As we get older, things change physically, but love transcends time. I've tried many times to picture myself aging as everything heads south. I'm hoping I find a partner before then, and one who will love me for my mind. So let's ask each of you your fears.

What for him is the one thought that scares him most about his body changing as he ages:

_____

What for her is the one thought that scares her most about her body changes as she ages:

_____

Now the flip side of this, what one thing scares you most about your partner's possible physical changes as they age?

His answer for her changes:

_____

Her answer for him:

_____

34-Looking only 10 years ahead sometimes is hard…where will I be 10 years from now? We gotta strategically plan our every move, put away for retirement and plan for what's ahead. So thinking up to your retirement what do you see you and your spouse doing at 65? If you're already retired, how well did the plan work out?

When we retire we want to:

Travel extensively _____yes _____no

Own my house outright _____yes _____no

Want to move to warmer climate _____yes _____no

Stay at home around the kids _____yes _____no

Enjoy hobbies more _____yes _____no

Fill in your own dream

_____

_____

_____

Now to do all that you start planning young. They say pensions won't be enough to carry us when we retire so let's ask you as a couple:

Have you begun to put away for that time _____yes _____no

Do you think you'll be ok when the time comes _____yes _____no

Are you hoping on a lottery between now n then _____yes _____no

Are you ahead of the game and have it planned _____yes _____no

If you've already reached the retirement age, a few questions for you:

Did you have to plan for your lifestyle _____yes _____no

Are you comfortable with how things are _____yes _____no

Do you wake up every day and enjoy your freedom _____yes _____no

Have you started any new hobbies _____yes _____no

Have you traveled to places you wanted to see _____yes _____no

All in all, how do you think your retirement is going? Was it everything you hoped it would be?

_____

_____

_____

35- You have been together a long while and I'm sure shared many fun times, but there must be a few occasions that just stand out as the best times of all. Think back, what one occasion topped the list so far? It was a moment that you both enjoyed every second.

What was that moment

_____

Who was there

_____

Where were you

_____

36- We haven't even touched on the sex life yet. Wow, what was I thinking? Now sex is an important part of any relationship. It's that wonderful bond that two share. So let's see how you view that side of your life. At times you have different ideals, memories of frequency or timing. Let's see if you're on the same page. His answers under M, her answers under W

33

The Sit N Do Nothing Series

	W	M
On average:		
How many times a month, do you have sex	_____	_____
How many times is it making love (There is a difference)	_____	_____
Is your partner a considerate lover always	_____	_____
The top 3 words to describe your sex life	_____	_____
	_____	_____
	_____	_____
If you could you would want sex how many days per week	_____	_____
times per day	_____	_____

My favorite thing about my partner when we're intimate is the way:

He _____

She _____

37- Think of your partner…I want you each to describe in 3 words your partner's sexual performance over the years… From the time you met until now:

He would say she is _____

_____

_____

She would say he is _____

_____

_____

Ok we'll take a break from that and focus on another part of life.

38-Don't know if you both work, but in this day and age it's hard to imagine only one supporting wage. So let's pick one word to describe your spouse's work ethic. Now we are talking the professional side, their job and not stuff around the house. Ladies put an M beside the word that most describes his style; men put a W which would define hers:

____Reliable   ____Workaholic   ____Focused

____Thorough   ____Puts in their time   ____Barely gets by

____Passionate   ____Driven   ____Minimalist

Who is the main bread winner in your relationship-Him _____ Her____ Equal____

39-Decision making as a couple is sometimes difficult. At times it can be mutual and sometimes one has the final say, but it's a balance between two people. So let's see how your relationship works on the decision side of things. Put the proper percentage that you each contribute to the following. Now remember each line has got to add up to 100 percent.

Big life purchase decisions are made:	Her _____% Him _____%
How to fill your spare time is more often decided by:	Her _____% Him _____%
Everyday shopping choices, foods, household stuff:	Her _____% Him _____%
Financial decisions-handling bills, payments, plans:	Her _____% Him _____%
Entertaining at your place:	Her_____% Him _____%
Travel destinations:	Her _____% Him _____%
Work to be done on the house/yard:	Her _____% Him _____%

I used to marvel at how mom could fill up our days with endless chores and such, she always had the plan. Dad followed along for the most part, but he had his strengths in the above as well, so I guess every couple finds their own balance.

40-The decisions regarding the kids are usually tougher and you both have a say, (they could be older now) but many times one decides more than the other. Who made the most decisions for each of the following (each line must equal 100 %)

Kid's activities-home: Her _____ % Him _____ %

Kid's education: Her _____ % Him _____ %

Kids clothing choice   Her _____ % Him _____ %

Kid's toys   Her _____ % Him _____ %

Kid's dating rules   Her _____ % Him _____ %

Extracurricular stuff   Her _____ % Him _____ %

Sport involvement   Her _____ % Him _____ %

Choices in friends   Her _____ % Him _____ %

Discipline   Her _____ % Him _____ %

Chores   Her _____ % Him _____ %

41-When it comes to cooking around the house I'm sure you've each got your talents in that department, so is there one special food that each of you is particularly good at making?

She loves when he makes _____

He loves when she makes _____

42-This question is on the sexy side and it applies to romance. Now use your imagination-if you could see your partner in any sexy outfit of your choice. Think on that for a moment- could be lacey, leather, vinyl, satin, silk…They have so many options for couples to wear, it could even be formal wear, nothing says sexy like a tux or sexy gown.

She would like to see him in

_____

_____

He would like to see her in

_____

_____

43-There are many fun things that just happen. Some people keep the spark burning with trying new and different things and some may not have done these. Perhaps some are on the list of things to try. Over your relationship have you ever done any of the following with your spouse?

Made love in public	_____yes	_____no
Swam naked together	_____yes	_____no
Enjoyed a nude beach	_____yes	_____no
Used toys with each other	_____yes	_____no
Role played	_____yes	_____no
Got caught having sex	_____yes	_____no
Had sex at the job	_____yes	_____no
Met midafternoon for a quickie	_____yes	_____no
Threesome	_____yes	_____no
Hot tub sex	_____yes	_____no
Had sex in the car	_____yes	_____no

Things just happen at times and some things add pizzazz to the sex life. We've come a long ways in life and are more open to trying new things. Are there a few you're thinking of trying now? (We won't get you to answer that one, surprise each other instead!)

44-You have a certain lifestyle and sometimes we hear about other styles or ways of life that just may peak our curiosity. Is there any one event you'd like to experience just once? You know when you get to totally dress in something you never have before and hang out in a different crowd-perhaps attend a formal ball, royalty, red carpet event, ride in a bike gang?

If you could, you'd like to experience just once:

His choice _____

Her choice _____

45-Now thinking back over history and the fashions back then. Makes you kinda glad we're born now, just picture how you'd look! Picture your mate in each of the following and on a scale of 1-10 rate how they'd look (1 being yep, their hot)

Roman empire	_____	for him->(hail Caesar)
	_____	for her->(Venus goddess wear)
Biblical times	_____	for him->(long hair/beard/sandals/sheet)
	_____	for her->(sheet and sandals for her)
Dinosaur day's	_____	(me Tarzan)
	_____	(you Jane)
Cowboy days	_____	for him->(hat/gun belt/spurs)
	_____	for her->(all bustled up-ouch!)
Medieval times	_____	for him->(armor/sword/chain mail)
	_____	for her->(Princess dresses were fancy back then)
The 50's	_____	for him->(the letter sweater/leather jacket)
	_____	for her->(bobby socks, poodle skirts)

If you were going to a costume party, what would you like to see your partner wear?

His choice for her: _____

Her choice for him: _____

46-Being a couple you've gotten used to each other's ways, a certain comfort zone. Depending on how long you've been together, things just seem to fall into place. The following are things that you seem to instinctively do because you know each other so well: Rate the 1-10 (1 being often, 10 being not at all)

_____ Finish each other's sentences

_____ One starts a project the other finishes

_____ Working on something together, you don't even ask to pass the tools anymore, your partner is handing it to you already

_____ Entertaining-your partner knows just when to show up to help with either serving, refilling drinks-you don't need to ask

_____ Grocery shopping-you know exactly which departments to find each other in.

_____ Hardware stores/building materials-you know before you even walk in which departments your spouse will visit, every time they go in there.

_____ You know exactly what time of day the phone rings and it's your partner

_____ When they're in a mood and instinctively when to just leave them be or when to approach.

_____ You can tell when they need to tell you something and are struggling with bad news

_____ You know where they put their keys/wallet/purse without even looking

47-You've been together a while if you've marked all #1's. If not, I'm sure it will come in time. Now thinking about how well you know your partner, you just know their feeling frisky and romantic when: (what is the one thing they do most of the time)

She_____

He _____

48-Now there is that one sentence that seems to mark every relationship- "We need to talk"! Yep, that's the universal sentence that we all dread, tis a sign of a bumpy moment. Please put a percentage, as to what most often that sentence is about:

Kids _____%

Money _____%

Relatives _____%

Work _____%

House responsibilities _____%

Romance _____%

Friends _____%

Health _____%

=100 % (Yep, it's gotta add up)

49-Seems with every couple there is one partner who has a better memory. Whether it's to stop and pick up the mail or milk on the way home, or where they stayed on vacation. There is one who seems to just forget about the details and little things:

He forgets more often _____   She forgets more often _____

Along with that there is the one who misplaces things quite a bit. I know I'll be wrapping Christmas gifts and I lose the tape 10 times while I'm sitting right there. So who is that person in your relationship?

He is _____   She is _____

Now watching my sister's marriage, her husband lost his bank card 3 times! I know he's not the only one to do that, many have done the same thing or lost jewelry…so who permanently loses more stuff?

He does _____   She does _____

50-When it comes to balancing a house, yard work, kids-sometimes you need to juggle back and forth. For the most part who does most of the following, not that they are better at it, just who ends up doing it most often? Put a W if she does/did it most and M if he does/did it most or an E if you both absolutely agree you share that one equally.

Cooking	_____	Dishes	_____
Wash clothes	_____	Fold clothes	_____
Vacuuming	_____	Dusting	_____
Washing floors	_____	Bathing the kids	_____
Driving the kids	_____	Dressing kids	_____
Feeding the kids	_____	Changing diapers	_____
Meal planning	_____	Grocery shopping	_____
Balancing finances	_____	Bill paying	_____
Clean the bathroom	_____	Washing vehicles	_____
Raking leaves	_____	Organizing house	_____
Packing for vacation	_____	Take kids to school	_____

There is a lot of stuff to get done, no wonder you're busy. Some schedules are just hectic, but it took partnership to get this far.

51-With all the stuff couples need to do, I'm sure there have been a few battles along the way. Nothing worth having is ever easy and life has a way of taking left turns when we least expect it. So let's see how you've coped:

The first battle was over _____

The worst one so far was over _____

The most recent is over _____

52-Guess we all have them. A lot of the time battles are due to in-laws-(sometimes outlaws). When you are in relationship or marry into a family-yep, you have a whole bunch of other people in your life. I'm sure you love your partner's family… it could be merely a different way of doing things or different ideals that set you apart.

So which side do you mostly hang out with

        His side____   Her side____

Now out of all the relatives on each other's side there is always one we get along the best with. Each must have a favorite to go see.

His favorite in-law is _____

Her favorite in-law is _____

53-We'll change the subject for a bit. When you and your partner look around your neighborhood how do you rate? You can only pick one here and you both have to agree.

We have our own style	_____	Nicest place on the block	_____
Keeping up with the Jones's	_____	We are the Jones's	_____
Cozy/comfy	_____	Could use some work	_____

On a scale from 1-10 (1 being the best in the neighborhood) how do you rate your home?

We are about a _____

54-Communication is the key for any relationship it takes time learning how to talk to one another. How do you feel the communication is between the two of you? I have thought of some examples during certain daily life situations. Fill in how you see your partner responding to each.

For the Women to answer:

You're out shopping together and she is trying on a new outfit for the Christmas party at his workplace. She comes out of the room and it's something that just looks awful and says-

"Honey what do you think of this?" How does your man usually respond: (pick most appropriate one)

Honest to a fault will tell you like it is _____

Fibs a bit cause he's afraid to say he doesn't like it _____

Blunt-no way that looks horrible-no sugar coating _____

Whatever you want- doesn't really care about it _____

For the Men to answer:

You've just got home with your new haircut, tried something different for a change. It's not the usual and it's out there. You walk in and say, 'Hey Hon what do ya think of the new me?' Pick the most appropriate

Honest to a fault-I prefer it the other way Hon _____

Fibs a bit-you're so cute-look at you _____

Blunt-Oh my God we're going back there now _____

Whatever you want-doesn't really care about it _____

55-Fitness and health-Is it a couple thing for you or more individual?

Who eats healthier	Her _____	Him ____	Both _____
Who exercises most	Her _____	Him ____	Both _____
Schedules fitness time	Her _____	Him ____	Both _____
Anyone take vitamins	Her _____	Him ____	Both _____
Who is ill more often	Her _____	Him ____	Both _____
Anyone smoke	Her _____	Him ____	Both _____
Drinks alcohol	Her _____	Him ____	Both _____

Eat vegetables daily   Her _____ Him _____ Both_____

Eating fruits daily   Her _____ Him _____ Both_____

56-Right now in all honesty my spouse could do the following: Women use the M and put how many you believe he could do and men use the W for how many you think your woman can do.

	W	M
Sit ups	_____	_____
Crunches	_____	_____
Jog	_____	_____
Bike	_____	_____
Run	_____	_____
Bench–lbs	_____	_____
Cardio	_____	_____

Well now, I wonder how close you are to the truth-Gonna test it out?

57-We all love bad foods like pizza, cheese, ice cream, sweets…yep got a weakness for at least one of them. Answer for your partner, you know that they just can't say no to:

Men, what is her biggest weakness _____

Women, what is his _____

58-Now thinking along those lines of favorites in life, how well do you really know your mate? Women will use the M column to put down what they believe there man's favorite is. Men will put down the answer they believe for their woman's under W. Let your partner fill them all out before you go and correct them. That extra line is to fill in the correct answer if they mess up.

The Sit N Do Nothing Series

	W	M	Correct Answer
Color	_____	_____	_____
Food	_____	_____	_____
Movie	_____	_____	_____
Pastime	_____	_____	_____
Fast food	_____	_____	_____
Restaurant	_____	_____	_____
Sport	_____	_____	_____
TV Show	_____	_____	_____
Snack	_____	_____	_____
Drink	_____	_____	_____
Music style	_____	_____	_____
Hobby	_____	_____	_____
Flower	_____	_____	_____
Gift	_____	_____	_____
Game	_____	_____	_____
Book	_____	_____	_____

59- Whew! That was a bunch. Some people know them, some people don't, but you learn as you go. So many favorites, which means there are things we just hate as well. Let's follow the same columns as the previous question but these are things your partner just hates. Remember, only correct them later!

	W	M	Correct answer
Food	_____	_____	_____
Breakfast	_____	_____	_____
Chore	_____	_____	_____
Restaurant	_____	_____	_____
TV show	_____	_____	_____
Reality show	_____	_____	_____

60- Thinking of all the reality shows out there (they're everywhere), from swapping wives and families, to living all in a house together scheming or surviving unknown places. Don't know if you watch them or like them, but if you and your partner were forced to be on one reality show-which one would you both grudgingly agree to?

_____

61- Well let's talk about the kids again. Parents always have hopes for their children. They watch them grow and blossom to adulthood. The foibles, mistakes and choices! At times it takes multiple tries for them to find their way. We were like that, heck-at 47, I'm still learning every day! I'm sure my Mom still shakes her head at some of my escapades, just as I'm sure your Mom still occasionally shakes hers at you. So let's see where you are with your kids: So if you have children,

                                                            Name

Is there one you just shake your head at a lot   _____

Is there one who seems to mirrors your habits of youth?

_____ mimics him (dad) and _____ mimics her (mom)

Is there one with any special talents _____

Is there one who you think excels in school _____

What about excels in popularity _____

Is there one that has an offbeat humor _____

Is there one that learns the hard way every time _____

Is there one that is spitting image of you- Him _____

Her _____

Kids-gotta love em! If you could write one thing down right now for them to follow for the rest of their lives, it would be:

He would say: _____

She would say: _____

62- Thinking back to your younger years which do you think lead the wilder life between the two of you?

Him _____   Her _____

Now along with that thinking, who excelled at school between the two of you

Him _____   Her _____

One last time, who was more popular in school between you both

Him _____   Her _____

63-If you could go back and watch your spouse at any age for a moment in time, without them knowing you at all…you'd like to see how they were:

She would love to see him at age _____

He would love to see her at age _____

64-Now, if you could go into the future and glimpse what your spouse will look like coming up…you'd like to see

She would like to see what he looks like at age _____

He would like to see what she looks like at age _____

65-Lets think on the finances for a bit. If you we're to win, let's say $50,000 dollars right now-it's extra money for you to spend as you wish-what would you buy? List a few here. One trick, you both have to agree on the purchase.

_____ _____ _____

_____ _____ _____

_____ _____ _____

_____ _____ _____

66-Now let's say it is 1 Million Dollars you won, I'm sure you've dreamed of that moment at one point or another. What would be the plan now?

Would you move where you live　　　　　_____yes _____no

Would you help other family　　　　　　_____yes _____no

Would you invest a lot of it　　　　　　_____yes _____no

Would you travel the world　　　　　　_____yes _____no

Would you buy more toys in life　　　　_____yes _____no

Would you put it away for the kids　　　_____yes _____no

It is fun thinking about that…winning a lottery how great would that be? I'm sure we've all thought about how much it would make life easier. Just fill in yes or no for how you each would handle it.

Do you think it would change who you are　　　her _____ him _____

Do you think it would mean more or less
headaches in life (less/more)   her_____ him_____

Who would you show off more   her_____ him_____

Continue to work?   her_____ him_____

Dance on your current boss's desk   her_____ him_____

Change the way you dress   her_____ him_____

67-Say you won that million, who would tell first?
_____
Who would you not want to tell about it?
_____

Count the number of people you'd help no matter what. You both have to agree on this since you both won the money.
How many people all together would you help? _____

68-Now growing up, you dreamed about finding the right person and settling down. Seemed like the easiest thing to do back when you were 15. Then again, the world looked a whole lot different at that point. Did you ever think it would cost so much? What have been the biggest eye openers (number them 1-16) #1-being you were most shocked about the cost etc…

Cost of vehicle _____   Education costs _____   Kids clothes _____

Fuel for driving _____   Cost of food _____   School supplies _____

Utilities _____   Income tax _____   Baby needs _____

Cost of a home _____   Toys/games _____   Renting _____

Insurance _____   Sports equipment _____   School activities _____

Repair costs _____

I guess if you did realize this all you're ahead of the game.

69- I gotta ask, are you happy with where you are? I know it's never easy and we all have ups and downs, but I believe people wake up a certain way each day. Could be stress from work, money or those moments when you are content in life. So what are your very first morning reactions? Overall, put in the percentage that you feel corresponds. Oh and by the way…it has to equal 100 percent at the bottom of the columns to get an overall view.

Her	Him	
I wake up _____ %	_____ %	of the time smiling
I wake up _____ %	_____ %	of the time grumpy
I wake up _____ %	_____ %	of the time frisky
I wake up _____ %	_____ %	just follow the routine
I wake up _____ %	_____ %	of the time unhappy
100 %	100 %	It's gotta add up

70- I think finding love is the ultimate in life. To find that other person who understands and stands beside us all the way is wonderful! It often pushes us to want to be better people. At times we need that push and we sometimes have to give the push back. Looking at your partner now, I want you to list 2 things that they had to push you at. It could be to finish school or a project.

She needed a push him to: He needed a push her to:

_____   _____

_____   _____

71- Looking back on all your years together, all the good and bad and what you've accomplished so far. I want you to list the top 3 things that your partner has brought to your life just by knowing them.

She has brought me   He has brought me

_____   _____

_____   _____

_____   _____

72- Love…it's something different to everyone and it changes over the years. That elated excitement you feel when young may change to comfortable companionship 10 years from now. What you felt that first moment morph's into different things over time. So let's see how you define the word Love. Look at this past year with your partner, circle what you both believe exists today in your relationship:

Honesty   passion   communication   integrity   friendship

Companionship   loyalty   support   caring   laughter

Dedication   intimacy   enjoyment   openness   excitement   spontaneous

Durability   flexibility   understanding   compassion   fun   sharing

Giving   sensuality   goals   faith   humor   reliability

It is hard to define where we are in life and we get so busy that we just may not stop to think about it during the busy schedule. If you haven't circled all of the words above are there any you'd both like to start working on?

_____   _____   _____

73- It's not easy in this throw-away society to make it through to the end together. It all comes down to how hard you are willing to work at it and what you're willing to give up, change and focus on. Do you ever wonder about life? Mark (yes or no) under your column if you believe in any of the following: (W for her answers, M for his)

The Sit N Do Nothing Series

	W	M
Everything happens for a reason	_____	_____
Do you believe in karma/what goes Around comes around in life	_____	_____
Everything is pre-destined so you are merely following your life path	_____	_____
Do you believe that you can change anything if you want it bad enough	_____	_____
Do you believe in faith	_____	_____
Do you follow a religion	_____	_____

74-While we're talking about faith in life let's do some dreaming, shall we? The ideal house we want to retire in would be:

In which country _____

Which city _____

We would live on/near _____

How many sq ft is it _____

How many bedrooms _____

I would love a balcony overlooking _____

My dream bathroom would have _____

75-Have you had a romantic get a way? Some people make sure to do so many times a year, while some can't afford to. If you won a trip for two anywhere in the world…all expenses paid, you would treat yourself to a romantic two weeks in:

_____

76-Now say you won a trip for 4, all expenses paid-well except spending money (they never throw that in do they?) Who would you more than likely take with you on this holiday if it were a weekend away to a neighboring large city?

_____ and _____

Would it change depending on the destinations? Who would you take with you if the trip was for anywhere in the world.

_____ and _____

where would you choose to go: _____

Now let's say the destinations are as follows, would your choice's change on who to take? Trip for 4 to:

Virgin Islands	_____ and	_____
Italy	_____ and	_____
Iceland	_____ and	_____
The Orient	_____ and	_____
Alaska	_____ and	_____
What about a cruise	_____ and	_____
Train excursion	_____ and	_____

Wonder if you picked the same people for all or did you have preferences for different places?

77-Do you have pets? How many _____

Type of pets _____ _____ _____

How old _____ _____ _____

Who picks up after it most: ____her ____him ____both

The Sit N Do Nothing Series

Who walks it most: ____her ____him ____both

Do you dress your pet ____yes ____no   Does it like to be dressed ____yes ____no

They say with time pets and owners look alike somewhat, so does your pet look like one of you

____yes ____no   Who _____

78- If you don't have pets how do you feel about animals in general. Just because you don't have one doesn't mean you don't like them…

H loves animals on a scale from 1-10, 1 being love em- _____

He loves animals on a scale from 1-10, 1 being love em _____

Is one of you allergic _____yes _____no

79- If you could see one animal live and in person, wild or not, you would most like to be close up and personal with a:

Her choice_____

His choice _____

Remember the choice above was up close and personal. Some people are just not comfortable with being close to some types of animals. It's a downright fear. Which animal, mammal, reptile, do you hope never to cross paths with?

She is afraid of _____

He is afraid of _____

Now with that question there are some everyday things that just freak us out. I know for me its mice! If there is one in the house, I jump up on a chair and phone a friend immediately. So what are you most scared of when you find it in your home?

She just hates _____

He just hates _____

80-Shopping! We all gotta do it. Yep food, clothes, tools, just about anything in life we have to go and buy. Now we have the usual stores we go together to, but at times when we run on our own we prefer other stores. So here we go: Ladies answer where your spouse likes to shop under M, and men fill in where she likes to be most often under W

	W	M
Favorite place to shop	_____	_____
Favorite thing to shop for	_____	_____
Home project store	_____	_____
Pharmacy you use is	_____	_____
Groceries are from	_____	_____
Spouse-buys too many	_____	_____
Thing to do at the mall	_____	_____
Most of my clothes from	_____	_____
Shops for kids mainly at	_____	_____
Best all time bargain was	_____	_____

81-Now we each have a way of shopping. For me, it's the get in, get what I need and get out. My sister (not so much) she likes to stroll leisurely through the mall. So you would define your partner's shopping style as:

His style would be _____

Her style would be _____

82-While we are talking style why don't we sum up our partners personal style? We have differing opinions. We may think we look a certain way, but others may not agree.

M=She would define her style as _____

M=He thinks it's more like _____

W=He would say his style is _____

W=She thinks it's more like _____

If you could take away one item of clothing that your partner wears-(could be the big bulky sweaters they always seem to have on or the skin tight shirts they wear too much…even those old beat up lucky boots they wear so proudly) what one thing would you like to see disappear mysteriously from your partners wardrobe?

Men would say she should lose the _____

Women would say he should lose the _____

83-Now back before you were married, think back to when you were dating and how much you'd fuss over your looks when you knew you were seeing each other. I know life's busy, but do you still go out on a date once in a while? They say that every couple should have date night.

The last date we were on was when _____

We went out and _____

Ok, if your struggling trying to remember the last date you had, it's maybe time to re-kindle the romance. Think about it, wouldn't it be fun to do something? Get all fixed up special just for the person you love? So you may not know what each other would like anymore, because you've been too busy with the house, work, kids…so here are some suggestions. I would like you to each check off what you'd be interested in doing. Maybe if you read each other's answers you could surprise your partner in the next week. (Positive thinking here)

Date Options	W	M
Romantic Dinner out	_____	_____
Picnic in the park	_____	_____
Movie night-(late show)	_____	_____
Roller-blade in the park	_____	_____
Country dancing	_____	_____
Live concert	_____	_____
Live theatre	_____	_____
Candle light dinner for two	_____	_____
Hot air balloon ride	_____	_____
Night clubbing	_____	_____

Walk/bicycle in a park   _____   _____
Walk along the shore   _____   _____
Amusement park   _____   _____
Bowling n beers   _____   _____
Rose petals on the bed   _____   _____
Hot tub n candles   _____   _____
Couples spa day (massages)   _____   _____
Ballroom dance lessons   _____   _____
Better yet: salsa dance lessons   _____   _____
Sightseeing/hiking   _____   _____
A long cozy drive (back roads)   _____   _____

No matter what you choose, you gotta make time for being the couple you are. Sexy lingerie, candlelight, soft music, even just spending a night curled up together with a good movie. Get cozy and have fun!

84-Since we're on the romantic stuff, has your partner ever surprised you with something so sweet and thoughtful? You know a post-it in your lunch kit, naked picture, bubble bath for two for example? How many times?

She has _____ /times   He has _____ /times

If the answer is yes for either, what did they do:

She has:

_____

_____

_____

He has:

_____

_____

_____

85-Since we're on that sexy topic again, let's see how you feel your sex life has been in the past 3 months. On a scale from 1-10 (10 being the absolute perfect) how would you rate your current sex life?

She thinks we are a _____ He thinks we are a _____

No matter what you put there, you're doing better than me…I'm single so it's a big fat 0.

86-Vacations apart seem to be a new trend for people to take some time away once in a while by themselves. Maybe you already live that way due to work or maybe you do vacation separately with other friends once in a while.

Her best time apart vacation was with _____ in _____

His best time apart vacation was with _____ in _____

Now for families, have you ever taken a road trip? We used to drive all over the place when we were young. Long distance in a vehicle sight-seeing…it was some of the best memories.

Have you taken a road trip with your family? _____yes _____no

If yes where was the best one to _____

If no, would you like to try one _____yes _____no

To where _____

I remember one where our companions actually left their kids at a gas station when-they thought they were in the camper-Oops! Do you have a funny story of your own to share?

_____

_____

_____

_____

87-Quirky things we do sometimes. The way we talk, expressions, sayings…we all do cute things. What is your partner's cutest saying?

She thinks his is _____

He thinks hers is _____

What is your partner's cutest quirky behavior? Could be the way he flips his hair, the way she bites her lip at times:

She likes when he _____

He likes when she _____

88-Stars and idols, the rich and famous, movie stars, rock stars...they're all over magazines, TV, radio. I think we all have fantasized about meeting our idol face to face. Seems there is that one who when on screen just gives you shivers. In committed relationship or not....we're still breathing so it's normal.

If your partner could sit down with one famous person and have a conversation with them for an hour who do you think they would like for each: (ladies under the M for his favorites, men under the W)

	W	M
TV Star	_____	_____
Movie star	_____	_____
Music Group	_____	_____
Author	_____	_____
Talk Show Host	_____	_____
Sports star	_____	_____
Singer	_____	_____
Business Mogul	_____	_____

89- Thinking along those lines, if you could see one of them totally in the buff standing right in front of you. Which idol would it be?

His choice _____ Her choice _____

Now I know you're in a relationship, but don't tell me you haven't fantasized a love scene with someone famous! If you could live out that one night with the Star of your choice you would totally like to be in that love scene with:

His choice _____ Her choice _____

You are probably looking at your partner thinking, huh? Maybe giggling a bit picturing them in that situation so let's put a spin on this one, who could you picture your partner with in that love scene?

For her I would pick _____

For him I would pick _____

90- It's easy to laugh and have fun thinking about things like that. Poking fun at each other is all part of partnership. Now what about the things you wished for. You must have had goals and dreams of how you saw your life from childhood. What were the original thoughts when you were 10? Did they change over the years? Think back to when you were both young children, you each had a vision of how life would be once you found the right person.

I wanted to be or work as a

His _____

Hers _____

I wanted to find my perfect partner and have:

_____ kids (His answer)

_____ kids (Her answer)

I'd of course drive a:

His answer _____

Her answer _____

And I'd have the following pets:

His answer_____

Her answer_____

And life would all fall into place with a little hard work. Now, you know those are kid's thoughts. I wanted to be a Vet, have 10 kids, the white picket fence with horses in the back to enjoy every day and live happily ever after. Ok, well I've been divorced, haven't found the right one, have no pets at all and the white picket fence needs fixing. I never had kids and I guess it's a bit too late to start. Plus my backside hasn't seen a horse since I was 17. (What was I thinking....!)

91- I know you're laughing at my outcome, but how'd you do with reaching for your childhood wishes? Right this very moment in your life:
I work as a

His_____ Hers_____

I have been married how many times: His answer _____ Her answer _____

I have this many children: His answer _____ Her answer _____

We actually drive: His answer_____ Her answer_____

Did you meet the mark on some of them? I'm thinking I should buy a cardboard cut-out of a man and a horse just to say it sort of worked out for me.

92-Well even though we don't often get our childhood dream, we do find our way to happiness. You've got each other and you've come a long way. Sure it's not easy and maybe it's not perfect, but it is wonderful to find that equal. So I want each of you to really think about dreams for the future. I know the world is tough, but hopes are what drive us forward.

What are your top five dreams for the next 10 years? In 10 years we will have succeeded at (top 5 and you both have to agree):

1-_____

2-_____

3-_____

4-_____

5-_____

93-Ok that was thought provoking, so here's an easy one…between the two of you, name the 7 Dwarfs.

_____ _____ _____ _____

_____ _____ _____

Did you get them all or did you have to phone a friend to answer? If there was two more Dwarves, pick a name to describe your partner and it's gotta end with a "Y" though because they all do:

Her name for him would be _____

His name for her would be _____

There's that kidding around with a smirk again-Smile!

94-Don't know if you both drive or not, if you do, is there one of you that is more comfortable behind the wheel? I know I've been in some cars that left me feeling the seatbelt just wasn't enough to make me feel safe.

Let's check your opinion of your partners driving. Rate using the following scale-Ladies rate your men under the M, men rate the ladies under the W

The Sit N Do Nothing Series

A=Always　　**B=Getting Better**　　**C=Come on really?**　　**D=Doh**　　**F=Fail**

Confident　　　　　　　　　_____　_____

Courteous　　　　　　　　　_____　_____

Calm　　　　　　　　　　　_____　_____

Let's traffic merge　　　　　_____　_____

Never fights for parking space　_____　_____

Safety first-belts up　　　　　_____　_____

Pays attention　　　　　　　_____　_____

Never texts while driving　　　_____　_____

No Accidents　　　　　　　_____　_____

Check before merging　　　　_____　_____

No speeding tickets　　　　　_____　_____

Keeps focus-changing radio etc　_____　_____

Never gets lost　　　　　　　_____　_____

Asks for directions　　　　　_____　_____

Drives sober always　　　　　_____　_____

Never back seat drives　　　　_____　_____

Well now, I'm sure we've all messed up at times.

95-Ever wonder about life on the other side of the tracks? I've worked my whole life just to get by, but I do wonder how life would be if I'd had went to school and gotten that degree. Seems I know now what I should have done back then-hindsight is always easier. So looking back, if you could go back and further your education, to do something you know you would have been great at:

He would become a _____

She would become a _____

96-Well your home I'm sure is comfortable. You've worked hard to get where you are. Whether it's a mansion or an apartment...it's all yours! If you could do one thing to your home, one thing outside or change one room inside and it was all done by a professional at no cost to you, what would you like to change or renovate?

You would _____

Now they had a show I loved about friends decorating each other's spaces. I tell you there is not too many I'd give carte blanche to decorating my home, but if you had to choose one couple to decorate your home you'd have to pick:

_____ and _____

97-Wow three more questions and your done...bet you can't wait! Well let's get to the heart of the matters for the last three. Life is a mix of so much: Happiness, contentment, trouble and sorrow-it's a mixed bag of everything really. It's all in how we choose to see it. I want you to reflect on the connection you have with your spouse. Every moment shared from beginning to now. Love is what brought you here so each of you list in one word the top 3 things being with this person has made you feel about yourself. Look at your entire history and then fill in the blanks.

He has made me feel   She has made me feel

_____   _____

_____   _____

_____   _____

98-People take a lot for granted in life. We get busy following daily patterns that we just forget about the meaning behind it all. We presume that person will be there always, no matter what! But life takes harsh turns and you can never plan what tomorrow brings. Take a moment to think about all the little things your partner has done for you. (folding your socks, cooking your favorite food, checking your oil etc…)

Honey, I want to thank you for the little things you do just because you know I like or need it done. I want to thank you for: W is for her thanks to him, M is thanking her.

W	M
_____	_____
_____	_____
_____	_____
_____	_____
_____	_____

99-Now that you've laughed and shared throughout this book I think you should promise each other to do one thing that you've both been putting off. We all have them: I'll get to that leaky sink, yes I will buy more lingerie, let's take time to get out on a date once a month or start going to the gym, take that dance class, renovate the bathroom-whatever it is...I think you should pick one thing your partner has asked of you and just follow through. Here we go again with that barter system you relationship folks have.

Her: I promise that I will _____

Him: I promise that I will_____

100-Last and final one! That is if you haven't thrown this book out the window yet. I truly envy you…you've found what works while those of use still search for what you have. Some of us may find it, some may never. If you had to pass on one word of wisdom to the single people out there, or anyone who is struggling in their relationship, it would be:

_____

There-done! Wasn't so hard was it? I do hope you enjoyed working through the book. It was my hope to get people talking, laughing, sharing and learning about one another. Seems in this day and age we don't make time for things.

There are other books in this series, all directed to different circumstances and different questions. I want the world to reach out to one another, laugh and simply enjoy life and who they are.

Wendy Proteau

Blessed with three siblings and parents who supported my hopes, I was raised in a small Canadian town, in an average middle-class family. Single at age forty-something, I'm still figuring life out daily. Being a combination of realist and dreamer, you can only imagine the confusion that goes on internally. Half of me writes a story with 'the happily ever after', the other half, edits the work and keeps it more realistic.

I'd never written more than a grocery list until 2009. It came out of nowhere as I sat at my computer following an idea. The '*Sit N Do Nothing Hamster Series*' is my way to bring us all a little closer in this technological world. The workbooks of self-discovery are a way to share tidbits of who we are, in the here and now. Each of the seven volumes, designed for a specific audience, asks the reader about their lives. I have many more ideas to expand the series. This hamster never quits! They are now available via print on demand.

Finding my inner voice, I decided to try my hand at a fiction. '*And When*' was written from September 2010–January 2011. Receiving many reviews, the story resonated, often bringing them to tears, laughter, and at times… needing a cold towel.

Taking months to edit the final draft, I began to miss that creative energy and '*Now What*' the sequel was started in 2012 and published in 2013. The story continues to place difficult hurdles, forcing the characters to veer from their chosen paths.

My life would be nothing without the people who have touched my soul. Friends, family, co-workers, relatives…have all been there through the good and bad. Everything takes hard work and nothing ever comes easy. Well at least not in my life. I firmly believe that karma plays an important role. It brings us the people we are meant to meet, challenges we have to overcome, lessons we need to learn and dreams we are meant to reach for.

The Sit 'N' Do Nothing Hamster Series

Unlock Your Hamster-Volume One
An introduction to the series

The Single Man Hamster-Volume Two

The Single Woman Hamster-Volume Three

Hamsters Unite-The Relationship-Volume Four
Dating, Married or Living Together

Heart Broke Hamster-Volume Five
For the tough spots of break-up, divorce or loss

The Gotta Have Hamster-Volume Six
Advertising and what you buy into

The Hospital Hamster-Volume Seven
For those in hospital or home recuperating

www.wendiann.com

www.ingramcontent.com/pod-product-compliance
Lightning Source LLC
Chambersburg PA
CBHW080529030426
42337CB00023B/4670